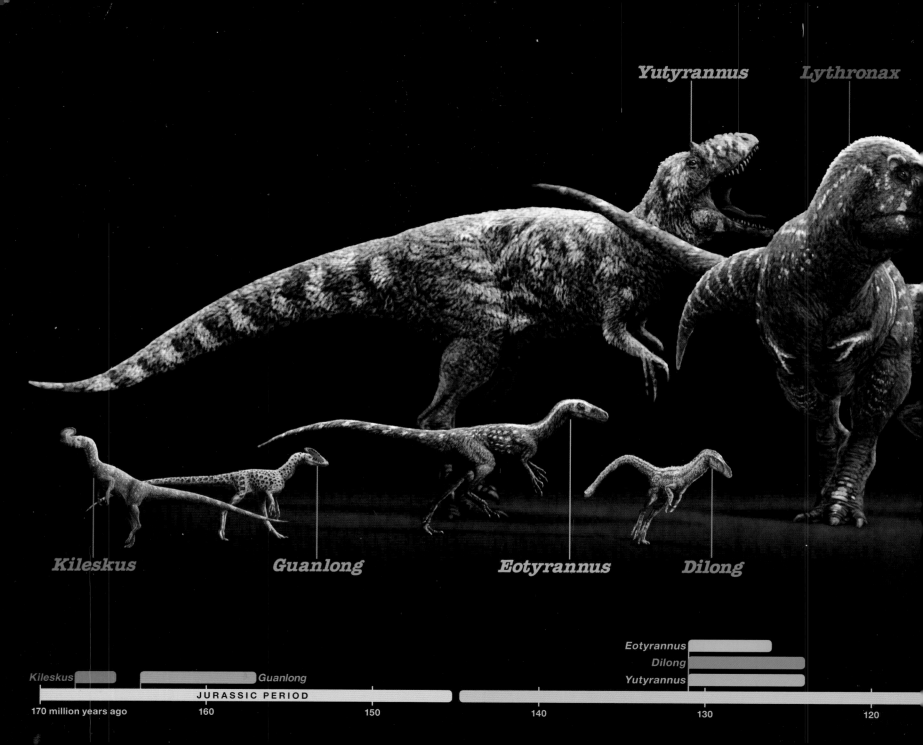

Yutyrannus

Lythronax

Kileskus

Guanlong

Eotyrannus

Dilong

Eotyrannus
Dilong
Yutyrannus

Kileskus

Guanlong

JURASSIC PERIOD

170 million years ago 160 150 140 130 120

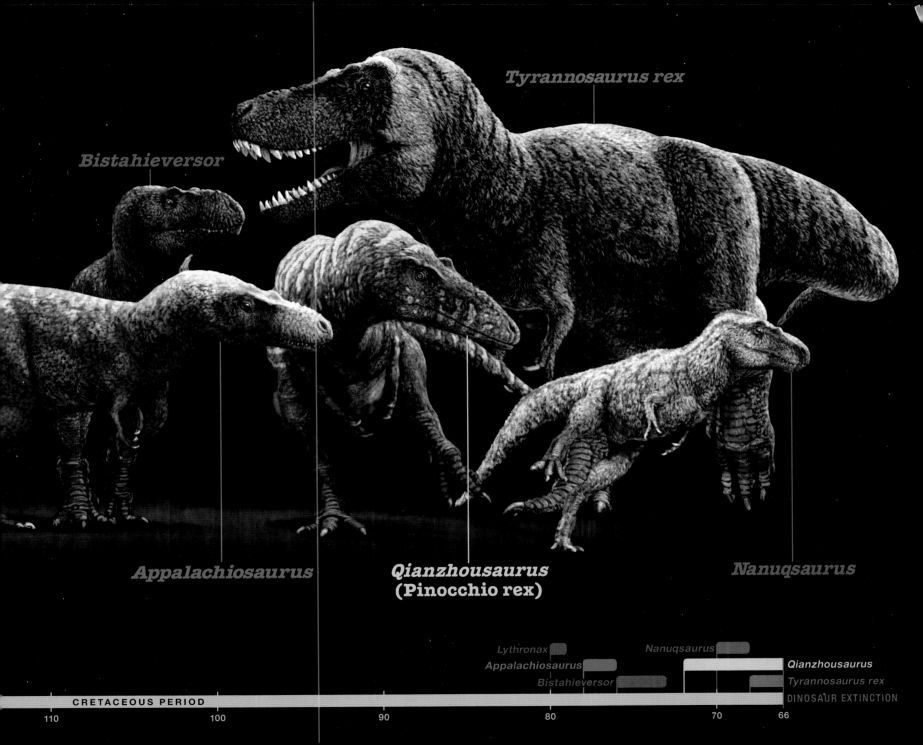

Tyrannosaurus rex

Bistahieversor

Appalachiosaurus

Qianzhousaurus
(Pinocchio rex)

Nanuqsaurus

Lythronax

Nanuqsaurus

Appalachiosaurus

Qianzhousaurus

Bistahieversor

Tyrannosaurus rex

CRETACEOUS PERIOD

DINOSAUR EXTINCTION

110   100   90   80   70   66

LEVEL **2** SCIENCE

LET'S READ AND FIND OUT

PINOCCHIO REX AND OTHER TYRANNOSAURS

BY MELISSA STEWART & STEVE BRUSATTE

ILLUSTRATED BY JULIUS CSOTONYI

HARPER

An Imprint of HarperCollins Publishers

For Steve Brusatte, a great scientist and
a great collaborator—M.S.

For my wife, Anne, and all of her fellow
school teachers everywhere—S.B.

For my wife, Alexandra, my joint adventurer
in life, scientific outreach, and art—J.C.

The Let's-Read-and-Find-Out Science book series was originated by Dr. Franklyn M. Branley, Astronomer Emeritus and former Chairman of the American Museum–Hayden Planetarium, and was formerly co-edited by him and Dr. Roma Gans, Professor Emeritus of Childhood Education, Teachers College, Columbia University. Text and illustrations for each of the books in the series are checked for accuracy by an expert in the relevant field. For more information about Let's-Read-and-Find-Out Science books, write to HarperCollins Children's Books, 195 Broadway, New York, NY 10007, or visit our website at www.letsreadandfindout.com.

Let's Read-and-Find-Out Science® is a trademark of HarperCollins Publishers.
Pinocchio Rex and Other Tyrannosaurs
Text copyright © 2017 by Melissa Stewart and Steve Brusatte
Illustrations by Julius Csotonyi
Illustrations copyright © 2017 by HarperCollins Publishers
All rights reserved. Manufactured in China.

Library of Congress Control Number: 2017932854
ISBN 978-0-06-249093-3 (trade bdg.) — ISBN 978-0-06-249091-9 (pbk.)

The artist used a stylus and a drawing tablet to create the digital illustrations for this book.
Typography by Erica De Chavez 18 19 20 21 SCP 10 9 8 7 6 5 4 3 2 ❖ First Edition

You'll meet a lot of amazing dinosaurs in this book.
Here's how to say their names.

Appalachiosaurus • • • (ah-pah-LAY-chee-oh-SORE-us)

Bistahieversor • • • • • • • • • (bis-TAH-hee-e-ver-sore)

Dilong • (DEE-long)

Eotyrannus • • • • • • • • • • • • • • • (EE-oh-tih-RAN-us)

Guanlong • • • • • • • • • • • • • • • • • (GWON-long)

Kileskus • • • • • • • • • • • • • • • • • (kih-LESS-kuss)

Lythronax • • • • • • • • • • • • • • • • (LITH-roh-nax)

Nanuqsaurus • • • • • • • • • • • (nah-nook-SORE-us)

Qianzhousaurus • • • • • • • • • (SHAHN-zhoo-SORE-us)

Tyrannosaurus rex • • • • • (tie-RAN-uh-SORE-us REKS)

Yutyrannus • • • • • • • • • • • • • (you-tih-RAN-us)

Why is *Tyrannosaurus rex* (tie-RAN-uh-SORE-us REKS) the most famous **dinosaur** of all time?

✔ Because it's so **BIG**. As big as a school bus.

✔ Because it's so **SCARY**. It had razor-sharp claws and teeth strong enough to crush bone.

✔ Because it's so **DIFFERENT** from anything alive today.

When the first *T. rex* **skeleton** went on display at the American Museum of Natural History in 1915, it took the world by storm. People had so many questions about **tyrannosaurs**.

When did they first live on Earth?
How had they changed over time?
Were they always so big?

10

For a long time, scientists didn't know the answers to any of these questions. But all that is starting to change.

What are we discovering? That the first tyrannosaurs were about the same size as us. It took almost 80 million years for them to become mighty beasts that ruled the land.

Dr. Steve Says

What's my favorite dinosaur? *T. rex!* I've been a fan since I was fifteen and helped my brother with a school project about the fearsome predator.

On a hot summer day, a worker climbed
into a backhoe and started to dig a hole.

Scoop.
Lift.
Dump.
Scoop.
Lift.
Dump.

The red soil slowly piled up.

It seemed like a normal day. But then . . . *Crash!* The digger hit something big. Something hard. Something the worker never expected. When he jumped down, he spotted giant bones. Lots of them.

When scientists at a nearby museum saw the bones,
they were thrilled. The worker had found a dinosaur!

The skeleton looked a lot like *T. rex*. But it was smaller and lighter. The huge skull had a long, thin snout with a row of small horns on top.

What was this strange tyrannosaur? To find out, the scientists asked tyrannosaur expert Steve Brusatte for help.

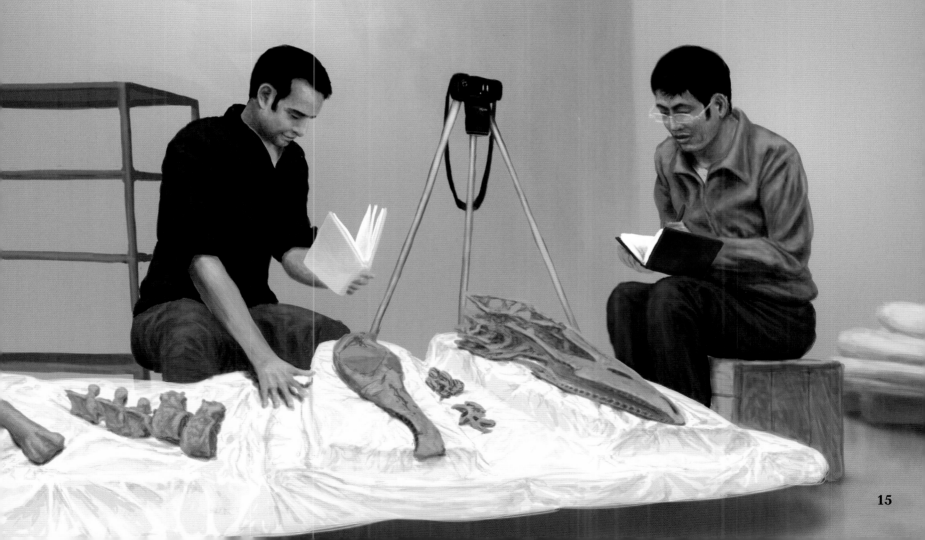

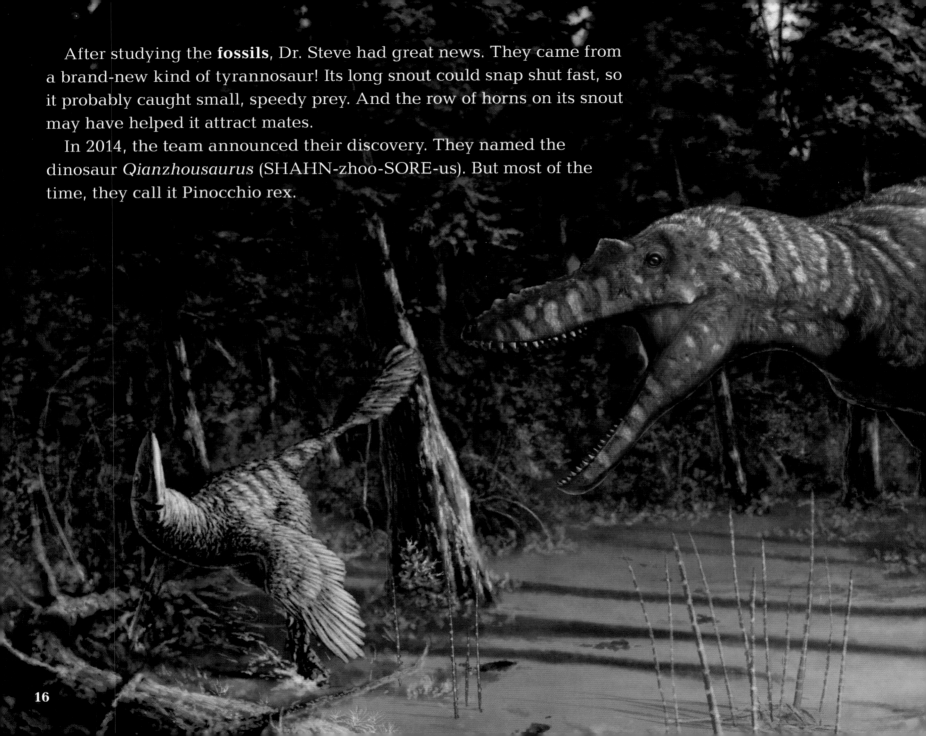

After studying the **fossils**, Dr. Steve had great news. They came from a brand-new kind of tyrannosaur! Its long snout could snap shut fast, so it probably caught small, speedy prey. And the row of horns on its snout may have helped it attract mates.

In 2014, the team announced their discovery. They named the dinosaur *Qianzhousaurus* (SHAHN-zhoo-SORE-us). But most of the time, they call it Pinocchio rex.

Dr. Steve Says

We named *Qianzhousaurus* after the part of China where it was found. But we thought it needed a nickname. The long snout made us think of Pinocchio's nose.

Pinocchio rex is just one of the many new tyrannosaurs scientists have discovered since 2000. Some of these dinosaurs lived around the same time as *T. rex* and Pinocchio rex, but others lived much earlier.

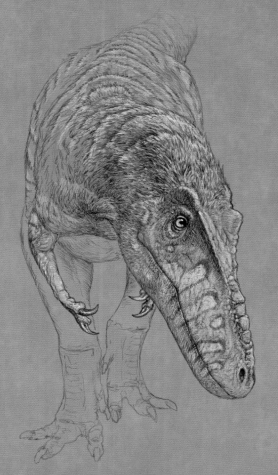

Kileskus (kih-LESS-kuss) was one of the world's first tyrannosaurs. It was small and quick. *Kileskus* had long arms with three fingers on each hand.

Kileskus

JURASSIC PERIOD | CRETACEOUS

170 million years ago   160   150   140   130   120   110

Kileskus

Discovery announced: 2010
Discovery site: Russia
Size: 9 feet long, 3 feet tall, 150 pounds
Lived: 168–166 million years ago

Qianzhousaurus
Tyrannosaurus rex
DINOSAUR EXTINCTION

PERIOD

00   90   80   70   66

Guanlong

Discovery announced: 2006
Discovery site: China
Size: 9 feet long, 3 feet tall, 150 pounds
Lived: 164–157 million years ago

Kileskus   Guanlong

JURASSIC PERIOD

170 million years ago   160   150   140   130

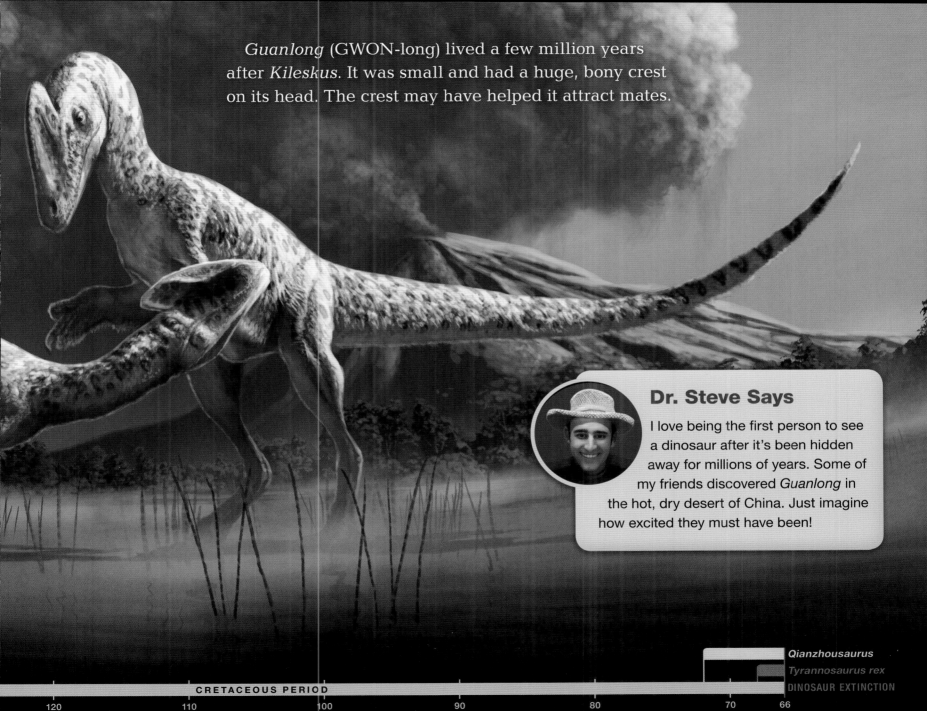

Guanlong (GWON-long) lived a few million years after *Kileskus*. It was small and had a huge, bony crest on its head. The crest may have helped it attract mates.

Dr. Steve Says

I love being the first person to see a dinosaur after it's been hidden away for millions of years. Some of my friends discovered *Guanlong* in the hot, dry desert of China. Just imagine how excited they must have been!

Qianzhousaurus
Tyrannosaurus rex
DINOSAUR EXTINCTION

CRETACEOUS PERIOD

120   110   100   90   80   70   66

Dilong

Discovery announced: 2004
Discovery site: China
Size: 5 feet long, 2.5 feet tall, 25 pounds
Lived: 131–124 million years ago

Dilong (DEE-long) is the smallest tyrannosaur ever discovered. Its lightweight body was covered with feathery fluff. The soft coat may have helped it stay warm. *Dilong*'s long arms made it easy for the speedy dinosaur to catch lizards, frogs, and insects.

Dilong

Kileskus   Guanlong   Dilong
                                Yutyrannus

JURASSIC PERIOD

170 million years ago   160   150   140   130   120

Yutyrannus

What did *Yutyrannus* (you-tih-RAN-us) hunt? Maybe *Dilong*. The two dinosaurs lived at the same time and in the same place. *Yutyrannus* was much bigger than *Dilong* and had long, hair-like feathers.

Qianzhousaurus
Tyrannosaurus rex
DINOSAUR EXTINCTION

CRETACEOUS PERIOD

110   100   90   80   70   66

Yutyrannus

Discovery announced: 2012
Discovery site: China
Size: 30 feet long, 8 feet tall, 3,000 pounds
Lived: 131–124 million years ago

Eotyrannus

Discovery announced: 2001

Discovery site: England

Size: 15 feet long, 4 feet tall, 400 pounds

Lived: 131–126 million years ago

Eotyrannus (EE-oh-tih-RAN-us) was alive at around the same time as *Yutyrannus* and *Dilong*. But it lived in a different part of the world.

Like other early tyrannosaurs, *Eotyrannus* had long arms. It could grab prey with the three long fingers on its hands.

Eotyrannus
Dilong
Kileskus   Guanlong   Yutyrannus

JURASSIC PERIOD

170 million years ago   160   150   140   130

Dr. Steve Says

A dinosaur in England? Yep, it's true. The first time I saw *Eotyrannus*, I couldn't believe it. The bones looked a lot like a *T. rex*'s, but so much smaller.

Qianzhousaurus
Tyrannosaurus rex
DINOSAUR EXTINCTION

CRETACEOUS PERIOD

120   110   100   90   80   70   66

Lythronax

Discovery announced: 2013

Discovery site: United States

Size: 24 feet long, 7 feet tall, 5,000 pounds

Lived: 80 million years ago

About 90 million years ago, tyrannosaurs began to change. Over time, they grew bigger and heavier. The giant beasts had huge heads with bone-crushing teeth. They had tiny arms with just two fingers on each hand.

Kileskus

Guanlong

Eotyrannus

Dilong

Yutyrannus

JURASSIC PERIOD

170 million years ago   160   150   140   130

One of these mighty hunters was *Lythronax* (LITH-roh-nax). It could catch and kill anything in its path. Scientists think that a dinosaur like *Lythronax* developed into *T. rex*.

CRETACEOUS PERIOD

Lythronax

Qianzhousaurus

Tyrannosaurus rex

DINOSAUR EXTINCTION

120   110   100   90   80   70   66

Over the next 20 million years, many new kinds of tyrannosaurs appeared. Pinocchio rex was one of them. So was *T. rex.* Here are a few others:

DINO FACT FILE

Appalachiosaurus
(ah-pah-LAY-chee-oh-SORE-us)

Discovery announced: 2005
Discovery site: United States
Size: 25 feet long, 7 feet tall, 2,000 pounds
Lived: 78–76 million years ago

DINO FACT FILE

Bistahieversor
(bis-TAH-hee-e-ver-sore)

Discovery announced: 2010
Discovery site: United States
Size: 25 feet long, 7 feet tall, 6,000 pounds
Lived: 76–73 million years ago

Kileskus

Guanlong

Eotyrannus
Dilong
Yutyrannus

JURASSIC PERIOD

170 million years ago   160   150   140   130   120

Dr. Steve Says

Bistahieversor was found in the badlands of New Mexico. I look for dinosaurs there every summer. I think it's one of the most beautiful places in the world.

DINO FACT FILE

Nanuqsaurus
(nah-nook-SORE-us)

Discovery announced: 2014
Discovery site: United States
Size: 18 feet long, 6 feet tall, 500 pounds
Lived: 70–68 million years ago

Lythronax
Nanuqsaurus
Appalachiosaurus
Qianzhousaurus
Bistahieversor
Tyrannosaurus rex

About 66 million years ago, an **asteroid** smashed into Earth. Dust from the blast filled the sky. It blocked out the sun for years. Earth became a dark, cold place.

Plants couldn't grow. Most animals starved to death. *T. rex*, Pinocchio rex, and all the other dinosaurs disappeared forever.

If it weren't for fossils, we wouldn't know that tyrannosaurs had ever lived. So far scientists have dug up about twenty-five kinds of tyrannosaurs. Who knows how many more are waiting to be discovered.

MEET DR. STEVE

I grew up in Ottawa, Illinois, surrounded by cornfields. My brother Chris loved dinosaurs. When I helped him with a school project on *T. rex*, I was hooked.

I studied my first dinosaur when I was in college. It turned out to be a new species. Since then, I've identified ten new kinds of dinosaurs. I've studied other ancient animals too. But tyrannosaurs are still my favorite.

Me at age 15, collecting fossils at Mazon Creek in Illinois

Me, age 11, (middle) with my brothers Chris (left) and Mike (right)

Me and my wife, Anne

Studying Pinocchio rex bones

Today I live in Scotland with my wife, Anne. She's an elementary school teacher, and I'm a **paleontologist**. I spend part of my time teaching at the University of Edinburgh. The rest of the time I travel the world digging up and studying dinosaurs. It's a dream job.

HOW BIG WERE TYRANNOSAURS?

T. rex was one of the biggest hunters to ever live on land. But many tyrannosaurs were much smaller. To see how tyrannosaurs sized up, grab three colored pieces of chalk and a tape measure. Then head out to the schoolyard or a local playground.

T. rex

Make a chalk mark on the pavement, and place a rock on top of it so you can easily see your starting point. Walk 40 feet to your right, and make a second chalk mark. Draw a line between the two marks to see how long *T. rex* was.

Now return to your first chalk mark, and walk 15 feet straight ahead. After making a second chalk mark, draw a line between the two marks to see how tall *T. rex* was. Complete the rectangle with two more lines and you'll see how big *T. rex* was. You may want to draw a figure that looks like *T. rex* inside the box.

Pinocchio rex

Using a different colored chalk, make a mark just to the right of the rock. Walk 25 feet to your right, and make another chalk mark. Draw a line between the two new marks to see how long Pinocchio rex was.

Now return to your first chalk mark, and walk 7 feet straight ahead. After making another chalk mark, draw a line between the two marks to see how tall Pinocchio rex was. Complete the rectangle with two more lines. Now you can compare the sizes of Pinocchio rex and *T. rex*. You may want to draw a figure that looks like Pinocchio rex inside the box.

Dilong

Using a third piece of chalk with a third color, make a mark just to the right of the Pinocchio rex chalk mark. Walk 5 feet to your right, and make another mark. Draw a line between the two marks to see how long *Dilong* was.

Now return to your first *Dilong* chalk mark, and walk 2 feet and 6 inches straight ahead. After making another chalk mark, draw a line between the two marks to see how tall *Dilong* was. Draw two more lines to create a rectangle. Now you can compare the sizes of all three tyrannosaurs. You may want to draw a figure that looks like *Dilong* inside the box.

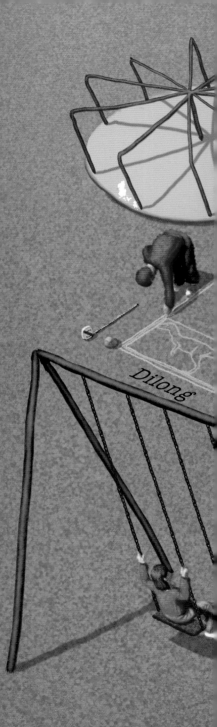

Dilong

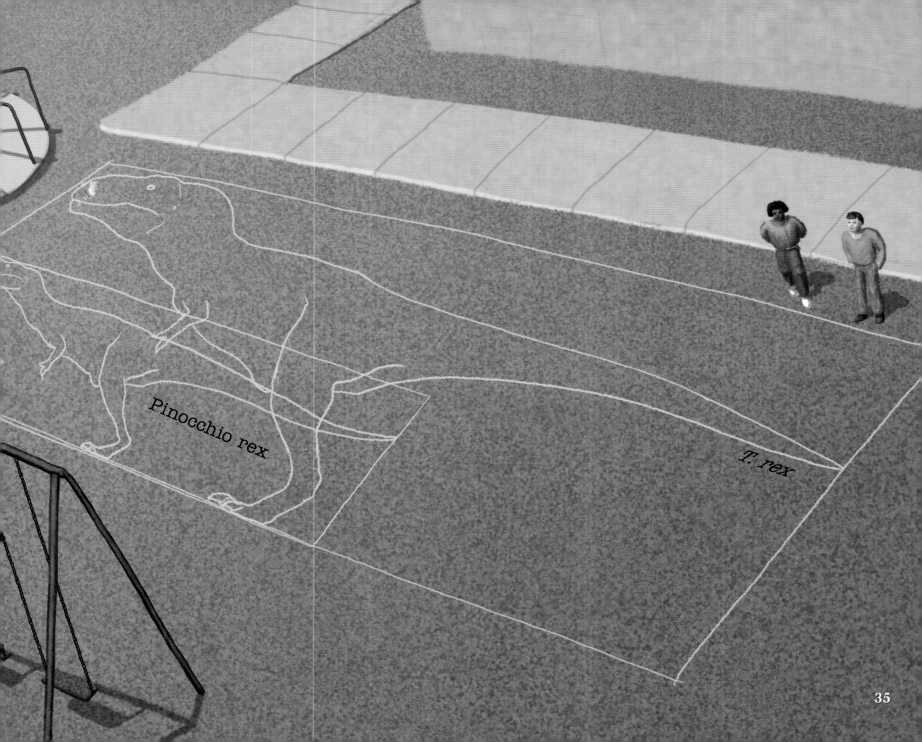

Pinocchio rex

T. rex

GLOSSARY

Asteroid—A large space rock.

Dinosaurs—A group of animals that lived mostly on land between 230 and 66 million years ago. They walked upright and had big arm muscles. The birds alive today developed from dinosaurs.

Fossil—Any evidence of past life, including teeth, bones, shells, plant imprints, footprints, nests, eggs, tooth marks, and dung.

Paleontologist—A scientist who studies dinosaurs and other kinds of fossils.

Skeleton—All the bones that make up an animal's body.

Tyrannosaurs—A group of meat-eating dinosaurs that walked on two legs.

WHERE TO SEE A *T. REX* & OTHER DINOSAURS:

← American Museum of Natural History, New York, NY
← Carnegie Museum of Natural History, Pittsburgh, PA
← Field Museum, Chicago, IL
← Natural History Museum, Los Angeles, CA
← New Mexico Museum of Natural History and Science, Albuquerque, NM
← Royal Tyrell Museum, Drumheller, Alberta, Canada
← Smithsonian Museum of Natural History, Washington DC

This book meets the Common Core State Standards for Science and Technical Subjects.

How TYRANNOSAURS Changed

KILESKUS

LIVED **168–166** million years ago

T. REX

LIVED **68–66** million years ago

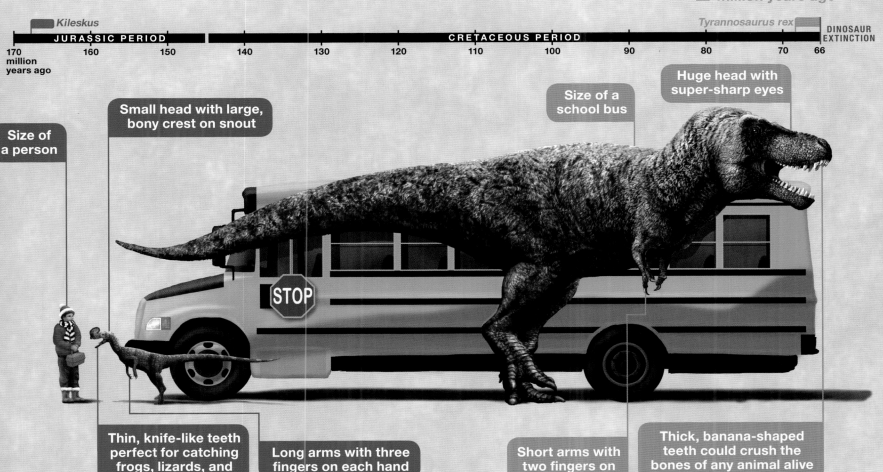

Kileskus

JURASSIC PERIOD

CRETACEOUS PERIOD

Tyrannosaurus rex

DINOSAUR EXTINCTION

170 million years ago | 160 | 150 | 140 | 130 | 120 | 110 | 100 | 90 | 80 | 70 | 66

Huge head with super-sharp eyes

Small head with large, bony crest on snout

Size of a school bus

Size of a person

STOP

Thin, knife-like teeth perfect for catching frogs, lizards, and small mammals

Long arms with three fingers on each hand

Short arms with two fingers on each hand

Thick, banana-shaped teeth could crush the bones of any animal alive

Be sure to look for all of these books in the **Let's-Read-and-Find-Out** Science series:

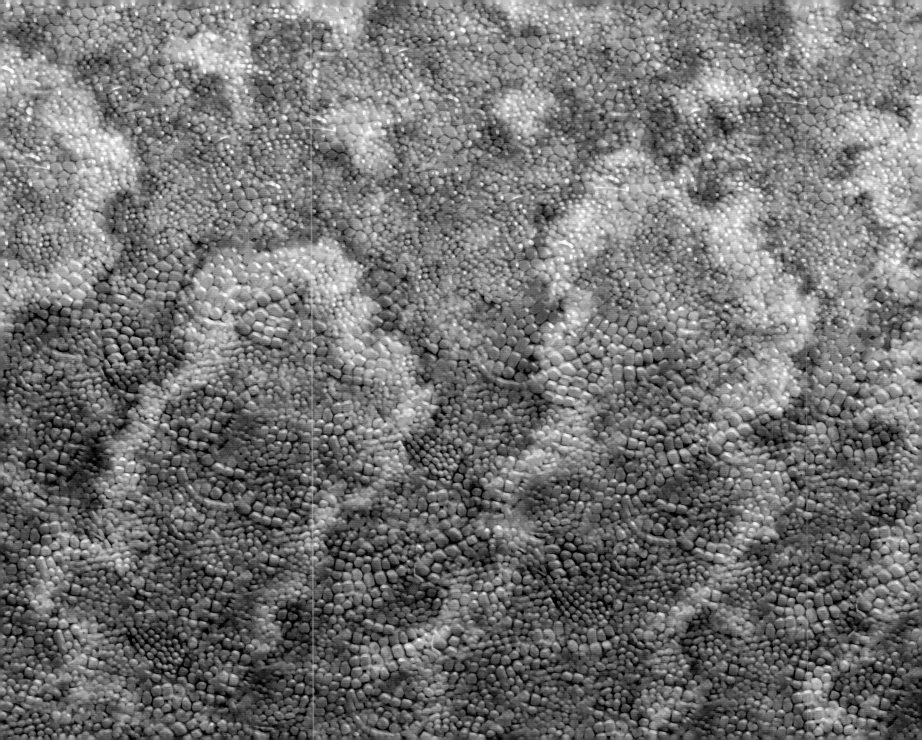